W9-AJO-623

Jewish Foods & Culture

by Jennifer Ferro

The Rourke Press, Inc.
Vero Beach, FL 32964

Note to Readers: The recipes in this book are meant to be enjoyed by young people. Children should ask an adult for help, however, when preparing any recipe involving knives, blenders, or other sharp implements and the use of stoves, microwaves, or other heating appliances.

On the Cover: *Young people in Israel dress up in fancy costumes for the Jewish holiday of Purim.*

Photo Credits: Cover photo, p. 22, 34 Steven Allan; p. 4, 10 PhotoDisc; p. 6, 13 Omni-Photo/Pawel Kumelowski; p. 9 Omni-Photo/Amos Zezmer; p. 12, 24, 35 A.S.A.P.; p. 17, 30, 42 Paul O'Connor; p. 23 Reuters/David Silverman/Archive Photos.

Produced by Salem Press, Inc.

Library of Congress Cataloging-in-Publication Data

Ferro, Jennifer. 1968-
   Jewish foods and culture / Jennifer Ferro.
    p.   cm. — (Festive foods & celebrations)
   Includes index.
   Summary: Discusses some of the foods enjoyed by Jews and describes special foods that are part of such specific celebrations as the Passover seder. Includes recipes.
   ISBN 1-57103-303-3
   1. Cookery, Jewish Juvenile literature.   2. Food habits Juvenile literature.   3. Festivals Juvenile literature. [1. Cookery, Jewish 2. Fasts and feasts—Judaism.]   I. Title. II. Series: Ferro, Jennifer. 1968-   Festive foods & celebrations.
TX724.F3775   1999
641.5'676—dc21   99-24327
                                                            CIP

First Printing

PRINTED IN THE UNITED STATES OF AMERICA

Contents

Introduction to Jewish Culture

The Jewish religion is called Judaism (JOO-dee-ih-zum). It has been around for over 4,000 years. Jewish people originally came from the *Middle East*. Their history is told in the Bible and also in the Hebrew Bible, called the *Torah* (TORE-uh).

The Jewish people have gone through many tough times. Many rulers have tried to get rid of them. In Spain, Jews were told to change their religion. Those who would not were killed. Many

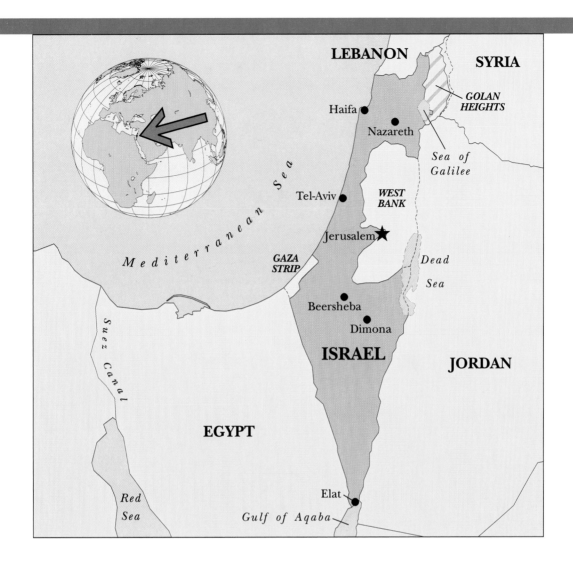

Jews learned how to practice their religion in secret.

In the 1940's, Jews in Eastern Europe were forced to live in prisons called *concentration camps*. Millions of them were killed in the camps. This is known as the *Holocaust* (HAW-luh-kost).

After the Holocaust, the countries of the world helped create a place for the Jewish people. *Israel* (IZ-ray-ul) is the Jewish state. It was created in 1948.

Jerusalem is the capital city of Israel. It is a holy place for Jews, Christians, and Muslims.

People who live in Israel are called Israelis (iz-RAY-leez).

Today, Jews live all over world. They are found in countries like Israel, the United States, and Ethiopia (ee-thee-OH-pee-uh) in Africa. They also live in Europe (YUR-up) and Latin America.

In ancient times, Jews spoke *Hebrew*. But people stopped speaking Hebrew and the language died. Jews who lived in Eastern Europe in countries like Poland and Germany spoke a language called *Yiddish*. Hebrew is now the official language of Israel. It is spoken by all Israelis.

Jewish people all over the world celebrate the same holidays even though they speak different languages. In this book, you will read about three holidays: Bar and Bat Mitzvahs, Purim, and Passover.

Many religious Jews follow certain rules about the foods they eat. Following the rules is called keeping *kosher* (KOH-shur). These rules are written in the Torah.

One rule is that milk and meat cannot be eaten

from the same plate. Families that keep kosher have two sets of dishes. One set is for meat like beef and chicken. The other set is for dairy foods like butter, cream, and cheese.

Another kosher rule says that chickens and cows can be killed only in a certain way. A *rabbi* is a teacher of Jewish law. A rabbi must see that chickens and cows are being killed the correct way for the meat to be called kosher.

Jewish people are also not allowed to eat meat from pigs, like pork, bacon, or ham. They cannot eat shellfish, like lobster.

Even with these rules, Jews eat different kinds of food depending on where they live. Jews who live in Italy eat Italian food like spaghetti. Jews who live in China eat Chinese food like rice.

The Passover meal is one way that Jews have passed their religion from one generation to the next. Jews can show other people how to pass on traditions and customs through food. You might eat food at your house that your grandparents learned how to make from their grandparents. Find out!

A young Jewish man prays at the Wailing Wall. It is the last part of the ancient Temple in Jerusalem.

Bar Mitzvahs and Bat Mitzvahs

A Bar or Bat Mitzvah is an important time in a Jewish teenager's life. In Judaism, this ceremony marks the date when a child becomes an adult. Many parents throw a party to celebrate this day. Not all teenagers have big parties.

In Hebrew, *bar* means "son" and *bat* means "daughter." Bar Mitzvahs are for boys. Bat Mitzvahs are for girls. A Jewish boy becomes an adult at the age of 13. A Jewish girl becomes an adult at the age of 12.

Until this age, children are Jewish because their parents tell them they are. At the Bar or Bat Mitzvah, teenagers take on the duty of being Jewish for themselves. This means that they will be responsible for doing the right thing. They become involved in the Jewish community. They learn prayers and how to read Hebrew.

At the Bar or Bat Mitzvah, the Jewish child reads from the Torah. This book contains all Jewish law and readings. The Torah is read at the *synagogue* (SIN-uh-gog). A synagogue is where Jews go to pray and to listen to their leaders.

Being Jewish

Being Jewish means more than going to a synagogue to pray or reading from a book like the Torah. Many Jews are not religious. They feel that they belong to the Jewish *culture* (KULL-chur). Jewish culture means things like eating certain kinds of foods and celebrating Jewish holidays. Some Jews do not go to a synagogue and do not know Hebrew. They still feel connected to other Jewish people because they have the same life experiences.

At a Bar Mitzvah, the 13-year-old boy reads from the Torah to all of his guests. He has been going to classes to learn how to read and speak Hebrew. He has learned about Jewish customs and holidays too. Then the boy must make a speech. It usually starts with "Today I am an adult." The speech is about how he thinks and feels about his new responsibilities.

The Torah is the holy book of Judaism. It is written on a large scroll of paper.

A boy is carried on his father's shoulders following his Bar Mitzvah ceremony.

After the religious ceremony, there may be a big party. All the teenager's friends and relatives are invited. Some relatives travel from far away to attend this celebration. Often, a band plays live music. The teenager's favorite foods are served.

The teenager also receives many gifts and sometimes a lot of money. The money is saved for a college education or for buying something very special.

Potato Knishes

1 onion

1 tablespoon of olive oil

5 large russet potatoes

2 large eggs

salt and pepper

1/4 cup of chopped parsley, oregano, or
   basil

1 package of puff pastry

◆ Preheat the oven to 375 degrees.

◆ Cut the onion in half. Peel off the skin
   and outer layer. Chop both halves into
   small pieces. Sauté the pieces in the oil
   until they are tender.

◆ Peel the potatoes. Cut them into cubes.
   Put the potatoes into a pot. Cover with
   water. Bring to a *boil* on high heat.

- Turn the heat to medium-low. Cook for 15 minutes, until a fork slides through the potatoes easily. Drain. Let the potatoes cool and mash them.

- Add 1 egg, the onion, some salt and pepper, and the parsley, oregano, or basil. Mash into a paste with your hands to make the filling.

- Peel off a sheet of puff pastry. Roll it out on a cutting board. Make it as thick as 2 pennies.

- Spread about 1 1/2 cups of filling onto the bottom third of the pastry. Leave 1 inch around the sides and bottom. Roll it up starting at the bottom. Cut the roll in half. Pinch the ends closed. Place the pastries on a nonstick cookie sheet.

- Break the other egg into a bowl. Beat it with a fork. Spread on top of the pastries with your fingers or a pastry brush.

- Bake for 25 minutes, until golden brown. Let cool a little, then serve.

Potato Knishes and Almond Roca

Almond Roca

The secret to making this candy is acting quickly while the toffee is still hot.

5 ounces of slivered almonds
2 sticks of unsalted butter
1 cup of sugar
1 tablespoon of water
12 1-ounce plain chocolate bars

+ Line a 9 x 9 square pan with parchment paper. Spray the sides with nonstick cooking spray. Line a cookie sheet with foil.

+ Chop the almonds into small pieces. Pour them onto another small cookie sheet. Bake on 250 degrees for 10 minutes. Do not let them burn!

+ Melt the butter, sugar, and water in a

pot on medium-high heat. Stir until it turns the color of peanut butter.

- Quickly pour the mixture into the square pan. Let it get hard but not too cool.

- Lay 6 chocolate bars on top. They should melt a little. Sprinkle with toasted almonds.

- Turn the square pan over onto the foil-lined cookie sheet. Peel off the parchment paper.

- Quickly add the remaining 6 chocolate bars on top. Sprinkle with toasted almonds.

- Let cool completely. Cut into small pieces.

Hamburgers

1 1/4 pounds of ground beef
salt and pepper
mustard
1/4 cup of mayonnaise
1/4 cup of relish
4 leaves of romaine or iceberg lettuce
1 tomato
4 hamburger buns

◆ Break up the beef in a large bowl.
  Sprinkle on a little salt and pepper.
  Squeeze it into the meat with your
  hands.

◆ Divide the meat into four portions.
  Form each part into a ball. Flatten the
  balls into patties 1 inch thick.

◆ Heat a thick skillet over medium-high

heat until very hot, about 5 minutes. The pan is ready when a drop of water sprinkled into it disappears quickly.

- Add the patties to the skillet. Cook for 4 1/2 minutes on one side. Turn. Cook for 4 1/2 minutes more.

- Slice the tomato.

- Place mustard, mayonnaise, relish, lettuce, tomato, and a hamburger on each bun. Serves 4.

Passover

Passover is a holiday that takes place in spring. It lasts eight days. Passover is a reminder of when Jews lived in *Egypt* (EE-jipt) as *slaves* thousands of years ago. The Egyptians forced the Jews to help build the *pyramids* (PEER-uh-midz).

The Bible says that God punished the Egyptians one night by killing their oldest sons. The houses of Jews were "passed over" and their children were safe. The Jews ran away from Egypt to escape

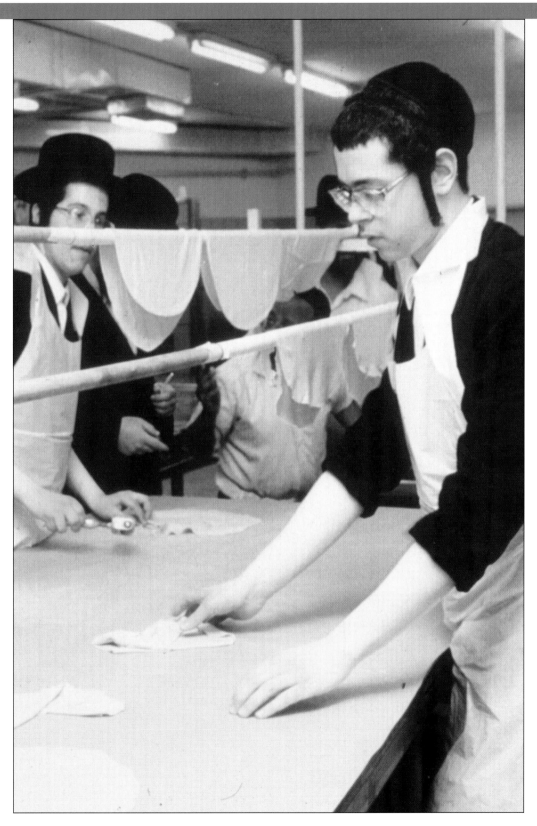

Religious Jewish students prepare matzoh.

A Jewish family eats the traditional seder dinner. The father reads from the Haggadah.

slavery. They had to leave quickly and did not have time to bake bread.

Leavening (LEH-vuh-ning) is the thing that makes bread dough rise. Leavened bread has had the chance to rise and get fluffy. To remember the escape from Egypt, Jews do not eat any leavened bread or cakes during Passover. They eat a flat cracker called *matzoh* (MOT-zuh) instead.

Jews have a special dinner on the first two nights of Passover. This dinner is called a *seder* (SAY-dur). A seder dinner is not really about eating. It is a way of telling a long story through food.

Everyone reads this story aloud from a book called the *Haggadah* (hah-GAH-duh). Six foods are on each person's plate during this dinner. Everyone tastes each food as the dishes are mentioned in the story.

The first is salt water. It is like the tears of the Jews while they were in slavery.

The second dish on the plate is bitter *herbs*. An

Elijah

During the seder meal, one extra place at the table is always set for Elijah (ih-LI-juh). He was a wise man called a *prophet* (PRAW-fit) who lived in ancient times. The door is left open for him too. Jews believe that Elijah visits every seder and drinks a few drops of wine at each house. Children watch the cup of wine during the long dinner to see if Elijah has come to their house.

herb called *horseradish* is often used. The bitter taste reminds Jews of the many years they spent in slavery.

A roasted leg of lamb is the third dish. This piece of meat marks the beginning of spring.

The fourth dish is called *haroset* (HAIR-oh-set). It is made of apples, nuts, cinnamon, and wine mixed together. Haroset is eaten as a reminder of the mortar or cement that the Jews used to hold together the bricks of the pyramids.

Greens like parsley are tasted as the fifth dish. They represent the green of spring and the happiness that comes when winter is over.

A hard-boiled egg is the last dish on the seder plate. An egg is where baby chickens come from. Humans too are born from eggs. People eat an egg at Passover to remind them of birth and how life goes on.

The real dinner begins when each dish has been tasted and the story is finished. All kinds of food is brought out from the kitchen.

One dish is called matzoh ball soup. It is made from crushed matzoh crackers. You can make your own soup from the recipe in this book. People can make matzoh balls as big as a baseball or as small as a marble. It is up to you!

Haroset

6 apples

2 plums

2/3 cup of chopped almonds

2 tablespoons of sugar

cinnamon

2 tablespoons of lemon juice

3 tablespoons of sweet red wine or grape
  juice

2 sheets of matzoh crackers

◆ Cut the apples in half. Remove the
  cores, stems, and seeds. Chop the
  apples into small chunks.

◆ Cut the plums in half. Remove the
  seeds. Cut the plums into chunks.

◆ Mix the apples and plums in a large
  bowl. Sprinkle on the almonds, sugar,
  and a *pinch* of cinnamon.

- Add the lemon juice and the wine or grape juice.

- Break the matzoh into small pieces. Sprinkle on the mixture. Stir. Serves 4.

Matzoh Ball Soup

2 15-ounce cans of chicken broth
2 eggs
1/2 cup of matzoh meal
2 tablespoons of vegetable oil
2 tablespoons of water
salt

- Heat the chicken broth in a pot over high heat. Bring it to a boil.

- Crack the two eggs into a bowl. Beat them with a fork. Add the matzoh meal, oil, water, and a pinch of salt. Mix with a wooden spoon. Refrigerate the mixture for about 15 minutes.

◆ Roll the dough into 4 balls the size of tennis balls or 8 balls the size of golf balls.

◆ Place the matzoh balls into the boiling chicken broth. Turn the heat down to

Matzoh Ball Soup and Haroset

simmer when the broth comes back to a boil. Simmer for 30 minutes.

- Spoon the soup into bowls with a ladle. Serves 4.

Matzoh Pizza

This is a way to enjoy pizza during Passover without eating leavened bread.

1 cup of tomato sauce or pasta sauce
1 cup of grated mozzarella cheese
4 sheets of matzoh crackers

- Spread tomato sauce and mozzarella on each sheet of matzoh cracker.

- Place the matzoh pizzas in an oven. Heat until the cheese melts.

Toffee Bars

This recipe shows that you can make anything with matzoh.

3 sheets of matzoh crackers
2 sticks of unsalted butter
1 cup of brown sugar
1 12-ounce package of chocolate chips
1 cup of chopped almonds

- Preheat the oven to 325 degrees.

- Line a cookie sheet with foil. Spray the foil with nonstick cooking spray. Place the matzoh sheets on the foil. Lay them side by side in one layer.

- Melt the butter and brown sugar in a pan over medium-high heat. Stir until it turns the color of peanut butter.

- Pour the mixture over the matzoh. Spread evenly with a rubber spatula. Bake for 10 minutes.

- Sprinkle on the chocolate chips. Bake for another few minutes, until they melt.

- Remove the cookie sheet from the oven. Use the spatula to smooth out the chocolate chips. Sprinkle on the chopped almonds.

- Refrigerate the cookie sheet for about 1 hour.

- Break the toffee bars into pieces. Serve.

Purim

Purim is the Jewish holiday where everyone forgets their troubles and has a party. It lasts three days. Special cookies, parades, costumes, and noisemakers go with this holiday.

Purim celebrates how Queen Esther saved the Jews from death. A long time ago, King Ahasuerus and Queen Esther lived in *Persia* (PUR-zhuh). Queen Esther was Jewish. One day, Esther's Uncle Mordecai heard the palace guards plotting to kill the King. Mordecai told Esther about the plot. This saved the King's life. Esther did not tell the King what had happened.

Haman was the King's trusted adviser. One day, Mordecai saw Haman on the street. Haman

Some girls dress up as Queen Esther for Purim.

expected all people to bow to him. But Mordecai refused and said, "I bow only to God." This made Haman very angry. The King gave him permission to kill all the Jews.

Haman put numbers into his hat to choose which day to kill the Jews. He drew the number 14. Everyone was told that the Jews would die on the 14th of March.

Queen Esther could not rest knowing that her people were in danger. She told the King that Mordecai had once saved the King's life. The King wanted to honor Mordecai. He had Haman killed

Noisemakers

You can make your own noisemaker for Purim. Decorate the outside of a paper plate. Glue on streamers or draw designs on it. Then take a handful of dried chickpeas and put them in the center of the plate. Fold the plate in half. Staple the edges together so the chickpeas cannot fall out. Jews call this a *grager* (GRAY-gur). Shake your new noisemaker!

instead. All the Jews danced and celebrated in the streets on March 14th, the day they were supposed to die.

Every March 14th, Jews all around the world hear the story of Esther. Whenever Haman's name is mentioned, they shake noisemakers and stomp their feet. Some children make crowns and dress up as Queen Esther. Others dress up as Mordecai. People also give gifts to the poor.

During Purim, Jews eat special cookies called *hamantaschen* (HAH-mun-tah-shun). They are shaped in triangles to look like Haman's hat. You can use the recipe on the next page to make these cookies yourself.

Jews also eat *chickpeas* during Purim. Esther lived in a large palace but never forgot that she grew up poor. Chickpeas are a symbol of Esther's childhood because they are a food that poor people ate. Chickpeas are used to make a delicious dip for bread called *hummus* (HUH-muss).

Hamantaschen

1 can of poppyseed filling, apricot jam, or cherry jam

2 teaspoons of orange juice

1 roll of premade sugar cookie dough

- Mix the poppyseed filling or jam and the orange juice in a bowl. Stir.

- Cut the sugar cookie dough into 1/4-inch slices. Flatten them with a rolling pin. Make the circles twice as big as before.

- Spoon 1 teaspoon of filling into the center of each dough circle. Pinch in 3 sides of the circles to make triangles. Do not cover the filling completely.

- Repeat until the dough and filling are gone.

- Place on a cookie sheet. Follow the baking instructions on the package of cookie dough.

Kreplach
(noodle pockets with mushrooms)

1 basket of white or brown mushrooms

1/2 onion

1 clove of garlic

1 tablespoon of vegetable oil

2 leaves of fresh chopped parsley or 1 teaspoon of dried parsley

salt and pepper

1 package of bread crumbs

1 package of wonton skins

- Chop the mushrooms, onion, and garlic into small pieces.

- Pour the oil into a skillet over medium-high heat. Add the mushrooms, onion, and garlic when the oil is hot. Stir with a wooden spoon for 10 minutes.

- Add the parsley and pinches of salt and pepper.

- Add the bread crumbs a 1/4 cup at a time to make a paste.

- Place 1 tablespoon of filling in the middle of each wonton skin. Fold over to make a triangle. Press the edges together firmly to seal.

- Repeat until the filling is gone.

- Fill a pot 1/2 full with water. Place it on high heat. Bring to a boil. Drop the triangles into the boiling water. Cook for 15 minutes.

Hummus

This recipe is easy to make with a food processor, but you can use a blender.

2 14-ounce cans of chickpeas (garbanzo beans)

4 cloves of garlic

1/3 cup of lemon juice (bottled or from 2 lemons)

3 tablespoons of *tahini*

salt and pepper

tortillas, pita bread, or crackers

◆ Drain the juice from the chickpeas. Pour them into a blender or food processor.

- Peel the garlic. Chop into very small pieces.

- Add the lemon juice, tahini, garlic, and a sprinkle of salt and pepper into the blender or food processor.

- Blend until smooth. Add a little water if it is too thick and blend again. Add water until the hummus is smooth.

- Serve with tortillas, pita bread cut into triangles, or crackers. Serves 3.

Hummus and Pita Bread

Glossary

boil: to heat water or another liquid until it starts to
bubble.

chickpeas: small, yellowish beans that are eaten
throughout the Mediterranean. They are also
called garbanzo beans.

concentration camps: camps set up by a government
for prisoners or refugees.

culture: a set of behaviors—including food, music,
and clothing—that is typical of a group of
people.

Egypt: a country on the continent of Africa that is
part of the Middle East.

grager: a noisemaker that is used by Jewish people
during Purim.

Haggadah: a book that tells the story of the Jewish
people. It is read during Passover dinner.

hamantaschen: cookies in the shape of a triangle
that are eaten during Purim.

haroset: a dish of apples and cinnamon that is made
   to look like the cement that held together the
   pyramids in Egypt.
Hebrew: the language spoken by Jewish people
   thousands of years ago and in Israel today.
herbs: plants with strong flavors that are used in
   cooking.
Holocaust: the time during World War II when the
   German government killed 6 million Jewish
   people.
horseradish: a strong herb from the mustard family.
hummus: a dish made with chickpeas that is used for
   dipping.
Israel: the country created for Jewish people. It is
   located in the Middle East.
kosher: a set of Jewish laws that state how certain
   foods can be cooked and eaten.
leavening: a substance that makes bread and dough
   rise.
matzoh: unleavened bread eaten during Passover. It
   is like a cracker.
Middle East: a group of countries that border the

eastern Mediterranean Sea including Israel, Iran, Egypt, and Saudi Arabia.

Persia: an ancient empire that is now the country of Iran.

pinch: the amount that you can pick up with your first finger and thumb.

prophet: a person who can tell what will happen according to what God says.

pyramids: structures in Egypt in shape of three-dimensional triangles. They are usually the tombs for Egyptian royalty.

rabbi: a teacher of Jewish laws.

seder: the traditional Passover dinner when the story of the Jewish people is told.

simmer: to cook on a very low heat.

slaves: people who are forced to work and who are not free to leave.

synagogue: the place where Jewish people practice their religion.

tahini: a paste made from sesame seeds.

Torah: a book of ancient Jewish laws.

Yiddish: a language that Jewish people spoke in Eastern Europe, especially in Germany.

Bibliography

Adler, David A. *The Children's Book of Jewish Holidays.* Brooklyn, N.Y.: Mesorah Publications, 1996.

Angell, Carole S. *Celebrations Around the World: A Multicultural Handbook.* Golden, Colo.: Fulcrum Press, 1996.

Bacon, Josephine. *Cooking the Israeli Way.* Minneapolis: Lerner Publications, 1986.

Berger, Gilda. *Celebrate!: Stories of the Jewish Holidays.* New York: Scholastic Press, 1998.

Kimmelamn, Leslie. *Dance, Sing, Remember: A Jewish Holidays Collection.* New York: HarperCollins, 1999.

Kindersley, Anabel, and Barnabas Kindersley. *Celebrations: Festivals, Carnivals, and Feast Days from Around the World.* New York: DK Publishing, 1997.

Kolatch, Alfred J. *Let's Celebrate Our Jewish Holidays!* Middle Village, N.Y.: Jonathan David, 1997.

Nathan, Joan. *The Children's Jewish Holiday Kitchen.*

New York: Schocken Books, 1995.

Webb, Lois Sinaiko. *Holidays of the World Cookbook for Students.* Phoenix, Ariz.: Oryx Press, 1995.

Zalben, Jane Breskin. *Beni's Family Cookbook for the Jewish Holidays.* New York: Henry Holt, 1996.

websites:

http://pilot.msu.edu/user/mille228

http://www.schoolnet.ca/collections/art_context/ holidays.htm

Index